GW00865034

Whales and Dolphins

Contents

First published in Great Britain by
Cherrytree Books, part of the Evans Publishing Group
2A Portman Mansions
Chiltern Street
London W1U 6NR

Copyright © this edition Evans Brothers Limited 2004

Originally published under the title
'Mes Petites Encyclopédies Larousse Dauphins et baleines'
Copyright © LAROUSSE/VUEF 2002
Copyright © LAROUSSE/S.E.J.E.R 2004

Text by Agnès Vandewiele, Michèle Lancina

ISBN 1 84234 235 5

A CIP catalogue record for this book is available from the British Library

Printed in France

ALL YOU NEED TO KNOW ABOUT...

Whales and Dolphins

Illustrated by **Nathalie Choux**

CHERRYTREE BOOKS

The giant of the deep

The blue whale is the biggest animal in the world:
it is as long as four buses and heavier than twenty elephants!

Whales belong to a group of animals called cetaceans.

Dolphins and porpoises are much smaller
than whales, but they are cetaceans too.

Mammals in the sea

Whales, dolphins and porpoises
live in the seas and oceans of the world –
but they are not fish!

They are mammals. Cats and dogs, cows and sheep, monkeys and people are all mammals too.

Fish or sea mammals?

What are some of the differences
between fish and whales?

Fish are cold-blooded animals.

Whales are warm-blooded.
Their body temperature is about 39°C,
like most other mammals.

Fish breathe under water.

Whales breathe at the surface.

Fish lay eggs.

Whales give birth to live young.
Baby whales suckle their mother.

Fish bones are very
fine and thin.

Whales have a thick skull, a
backbone and even a ribcage.

Recognising shapes

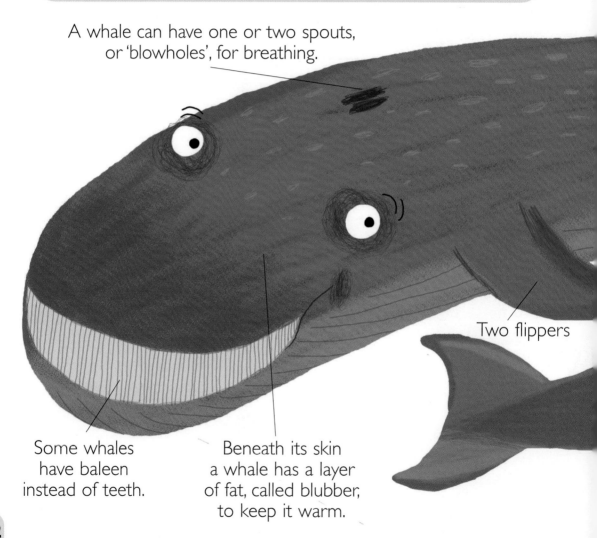

A whale can have one or two spouts, or 'blowholes', for breathing.

Two flippers

Some whales have baleen instead of teeth.

Beneath its skin a whale has a layer of fat, called blubber, to keep it warm.

Whales and dolphins have a streamlined body
and smooth skin to slip through the water.
They breathe with their lungs.

Dolphins have only one spout.

Two flippers

Dolphins, and some
whales, have teeth.

13

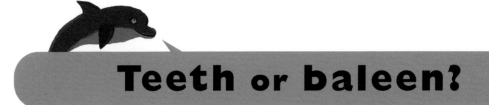

Teeth or baleen?

There are two big groups of cetaceans:
those with teeth, like sperm whales,
dolphins and porpoises…

…and those that have plates
of baleen, or 'whalebone',
instead of teeth.

Plates of baleen are fine strips of bone-like material, like a giant comb, which whales use to catch their food.

Cetaceans with **baleen**

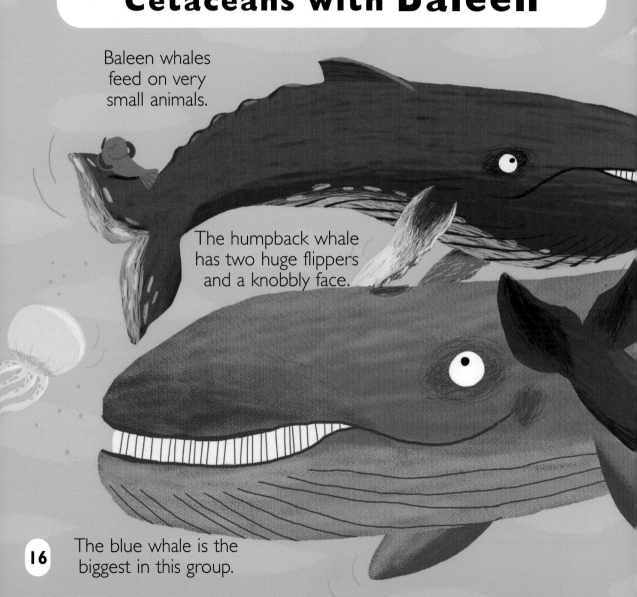

Baleen whales feed on very small animals.

The humpback whale has two huge flippers and a knobbly face.

The blue whale is the biggest in this group.

The grey whale is... grey, with pale patches.

The right whale has a big chin, often with barnacles on it.

17

Cetaceans with teeth

Cetaceans with teeth feed on fish, squid and all kinds of large prey.

Dolphins have a long 'beak' and a rounded head.

Common dolphin

Spectacled porpoise

Porpoises are smaller and have no beak.

The beaked whale has a long beak.

The narwhal has a long ivory tusk.

The beluga is white but its young are grey.

The killer whale is actually a large dolphin.

The sperm whale has a huge head.

19

Breathing, swimming and diving

Whales and dolphins rise to the surface regularly to breathe.

They blow out old air in a spout of water and breathe in fresh air.

20

Humpback whales are named after the way they arch their back when they dive. They sometimes leap out of the water on their back before splashing down again.

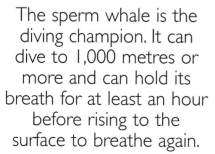

The sperm whale is the diving champion. It can dive to 1,000 metres or more and can hold its breath for at least an hour before rising to the surface to breathe again.

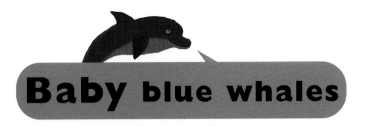

Baby blue whales

A female blue whale may give birth
to twelve calves in her lifetime.
She looks after her young on her own.

22

The calf is born tail first, so it does not drown before it can reach the surface.

When it is first born, it is bigger than an elephant!

It quickly swims to the surface to breathe.

It feeds on its mother's milk and grows very quickly.

The baby whale likes playing with its mother, sliding down her fins, wriggling on her back and cuddling up to her.

Baby dolphins

When a dolphin gives birth, another dolphin, called the godmother, sometimes helps.

The baby dolphin sucks milk from its mother until its teeth grow.

The mother and the godmother help the new baby dolphin to reach the surface to breathe.

Dolphins stay in family groups, called pods.

If danger threatens, the baby hides under its mother's stomach.

A long journey

Whales spend the summer in colder waters, where they eat a lot.

They eat as much as possible to build up reserves of fat for the long journey ahead.

In the winter, they swim thousands of kilometres to reach warmer waters, where they give birth. They don't eat very much.

Eating habits

Some of the biggest animals in the world eat some of the smallest!

Dolphins eat fish, shellfish, octopus, cuttlefish…. They catch them with their teeth and swallow them whole, without chewing them.

The killer whale uses its teeth to tear up its food – usually fish and squid.

The sperm whale dives very deep to find its favourite food: giant squid.

Baleen whales take in huge mouthfuls of water containing
thousands of tiny shrimp-like krill, then they close their mouth
and push out the water, trapping the krill behind the baleen plates.

Sounds in the water

Dolphins make noises that people cannot hear.

The noises are clicking sounds. If a dolphin makes a distress signal, other dolphins go to its rescue.

Male whales sing
in the water.

The beluga whale warbles
and whistles like a bird.
It is called the 'sea canary'.

Whales give out sounds
that other whales can hear
a long way away.

The narwhal makes
sharp cries.

The real acrobats

Whales can jump far out of the water.
They leap high, then fall back into the water
on their backs, making a huge splash.

Dolphins are the real champions of jumping and twirling.

They surf the waves as they follow ships through the water.

They leap and dive as they swim along. It's a wonderful sight!

Whale alert!

For thousands of years, people hunted whales,
mostly for meat and fat.
The whale was harpooned and towed to the side of the ship.

Today, whales are protected,
and almost all whale hunting is forbidden.

Whale fat was used to make soap and candles.
Baleen was used in ladies' clothes and to make brushes.

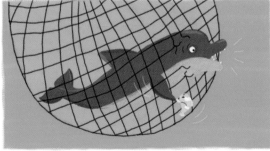

Today, dolphins are threatened by pollution of the seas.
And they often get caught in fishing nets.

Records

The **biggest**

The blue whale is the biggest and heaviest animal in the world.

The biggest **heart**

The blue whale's heart is as big as a small car.

The heaviest **tongue**

Its tongue weighs as much as an elephant!

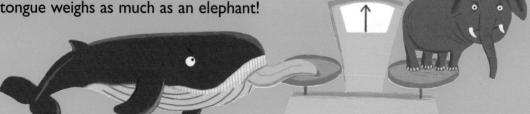

The most **teeth**

Some dolphins can have more than 200 teeth – ten times more than a child has.

The biggest **mouth**

Baleen whales have huge mouths, which could hold a small house.

The best **diver**

The sperm whale can dive for an hour and a half without breathing.

The most **musical**

When the humpback whale sings, it can make more than a thousand different sounds.

Index